First published in Great Britain in 1997 by
POETRY NOW
1-2 Wainman Road, Woodston,
Peterborough, PE2 7BU
Telephone (01733) 230746
Fax (01733) 230751

HB ISBN 1 86188 516 4
SB ISBN 1 86188 511 3

FOREWORD

Although we are a nation of poetry writers we are accused of not reading poetry and not buying poetry books: after many years of listening to the incessant gripes of poetry publishers, I can only assume that the books they publish, in general, are books that most people do not want to read.

Poetry should not be obscure, introverted, and as cryptic as a crossword puzzle: it is the poet's duty to reach out and embrace the world.

The world owes the poet nothing and we should not be expected to dig and delve into a rambling discourse searching for some inner meaning.

The reason we write poetry (and almost all of us do) is because we want to communicate: an ideal; an idea; or a specific feeling. Poetry is as essential in communication, as a letter; a radio; a telephone, and the main criteria for selecting the poems in this anthology is very simple: they communicate.

Faced with hundreds of poems and a limited amount of space, the task of choosing the final poems was difficult and as editor one tries to be as detached as possible (quite often editors can become a barrier in the writer-reader exchange) acting as go between, making the connection, not censoring because of personal taste.

Homelessness is one of many issues today which is easily ignored or forgotten. How many times have you walked down the street and seen a homeless person but just carried on walking without giving a single thought to how life must be for them? And many people don't think twice about putting spare change in a charity box yet don't even consider buying a copy of 'The Big Issue'.

This anthology has brought together all the issues of homelessness in a poetical form. The poems are written by everyday people who have voiced their opinions on the homeless. Through their writing the poets have come together and presented the problem as it stands today, a problem which we all should know about and be aware of.

The success of this collection, and all previous *Poetry Now* anthologies, relies on the fact that there are as many individual readers as there are writers

CONTENTS

STREET LIFE

I was down and out without a doubt
Parents gone, family too,
What in God's name was I to do?
The streets were cold the jacket was old -
The shoes had seen better days -
My mother often used to say you'd better
Mend your ways, your brothers and sisters -
Have done real good, why is it you -
Are misunderstood.
I walked on, cold and tired, saw a church -
Hall, with lights on, inside, could I ask
To sleep upon the floor? I had done it
Once before, I plucked up courage
And knocked on the door went in and
Sat on a chair, the caretaker said do
You want a bite to eat, you can then have a
Sleep before you go on your way, I was taken
A back by this kindness, I could feel my mother's
Shame, and in the days gone, by I could hear her
Say 'Stand up when your spoken to and take your
Hands out of your pockets' I thanked that man,
There and then and said I'd make good and
See him again, years have gone by, hard and
Cold but I pushed on and I'm not
Too old, I've a roof over my head and
A decent bed and a wee job to earn my
Daily bread.
Who knows we may all meet up again,
I am thankful to that man in that church
Hall who gave me a chance to try again.

Janet Fletcher

CAN YOU SPARE SOME CHANGE PLEASE

Dirty blankets cover their legs
As using their signs they silently beg
Hungry and homeless, jobless and poor
Please Mr Businessman can you spare some more

Sheltered in doorways, huddled on stairs
Trolleys and bags holding their wears
Drunk and old, toothless and hairy
Young and scared, bitter and weary

On every station on the underground
In every dark corner, on streets all around
Talking together or sat quiet and hurt
They're matted and stinking, covered in dirt

They're scorned and spat on, laughed at and blamed
A living indication of how our world's changed
They're losers of life, or politics gone wrong
Whatever you think, you can't block out their song

We pass them our pennies and pass off our guilt
Cold and cynical to survive this world we have built
We accuse them of alcohol, theft and drugs
We believe that they're con-men, stupid or thugs

How can we stop this downward slope
How can we make nothing turn into hope
What is the answer, does anyone know
We can't close our eyes and hope that they'll go.

Fay Jenkinson

LIFE ON THE STREET

Darkness creeps in I walk around
until a place to sleep I have found
   Same situation, a bench in the park
I am so scared alone, and fear the dark

No-one wants me, I'm a down and out
   I just want to stand up and shout
What's wrong with the world does no-one care
For all the homeless people who live in fear
of being raped and attacked and even mugged
   All I want is to be loved.

So come on you government
   wake up to the fact
that you have been careless
   And very slack
So change the rules and then you will see
what a better world this will be.

Irene Joan Blair

A PLEA FOR THE HOMELESS

I'm a vagrant, the street pavement
Is my only home, there are some
People, who pass me by, and never cast an eye
In my direction, if I should live or die
To them it matters little.

We're homeless, the young and old
Suffering from the damp and cold
Thirsty, hungry, in our pockets no money
Limbs stiff, head aching, unloved our hearts breaking
Perhaps a criminal in the making.

You who have homes, don't you care?
Cannot you spare a thought for me
Huddled in a doorway in cold's intensity?
Politicians, stinking rich, if you saw me in a ditch
About to drown, you would simply walk on, out of town.

Some of us were once like you
In houses with a lovely view
A weekly wage, friends by the score
We were content, and sought no more
Somewhere along the way, our good luck went astray
Little by little, we lost everything
But kept on hoping our good name
Would not suffer further shame.

In society today, there ought to be a way
To provide a home for everyone
The homeless man needs security
Shelter for his body, and dignity
Not much to ask, it seems to me
But beyond our country's scope
To give these people such a hope.

Marjorie Walshe

STREET LIFE

I think that the government should wake up.
To the plight of the homeless,
Because all over the country,
The situation is just a mess.

Instead of fighting amongst themselves.
They should stop and think for a while,
They should think of some desolate soul,
Who has no reason to smile.

Put your minds together,
And think what you should do.
Only they should thank themselves,
It is not happening to you.

Let's have some cash from the lottery
To enable us to build homes,
For then those unfortunate,
The streets they would not roam.

Then they could put a feather,
In their thinking caps,
For the proudness of the country,
And the happiness they get from that.

M E Farr

PROSTITUTE

The lady on the corner
waiting for a client
fag in hand swinging bag
the law to be defiant

Choose your favourite condom
there's blue pink or green
She'll make your eyes water
or in agony you'll scream

You can have a bit of bondage
or simply good old sex
but if you prefer adventure
you'll find her never vex

Fifty pound a blow job
thirty pound the rest
it's just an occupation
only she does best.

Linda Shropshire

THE BAG LADY

Movement by the dustbins - A bulging aged crone!
Matted hair - Bleary eyes - Leather covered bone!

Emerging from her rotting bed,
To feed a need inside her head!

Stumbling - Lurching - Ransacking bins!
Frantically searching - Peering in tins!

Suddenly she holds a prize!
Excitement in her bloodshot eyes.

A half-full can - -Stinking - Rank!
With a thirst to kill - It's quickly drank!

A victim of society? - It knows but doesn't care!
The bag lady can't tell us - Her mind's no longer there.

In this way of life she's found some space,
Just another soul lost in the human race.

Colin Needham

LONELY SPIRITS

Somewhere a dog barks,
In a cold, empty street.
Dreaming of running,
It has sores on its feet.

Somewhere a dog howls,
Crying out to be heard,
As it sits on its own,
Alone in the world.

Somewhere a dog
Stares up at the stars,
Wishing to fly
Out of this dark.

Somewhere a dog
Cries tears of pain,
Wanting someone to love,
To be loved once again.

Somewhere, a girl,
Alone in the cold,
Lays down her head,
Her dreams she unfolds.

Somewhere a dog,
With hope in its eyes,
Sees a girl,
And beside her lies.

Somewhere the girl loves,
Happy again,
Somewhere the dog,
Is safe with a friend.

Sara Ingham

N'OME

(For the homeless who live in cardboard cities)

I've got a n'ome and I'm proud of it.
Me 'ome's me castle, though it's cramped a bit.
          The walls are very thin,
There's no running water and no electric light,
But me 'ome keeps me warm on cold dark nights.
          Sometimes the rain comes in.

When the wind blows litter through the streets,
Me 'ome's me shelter, the place where I sleep.
          I'm comfortable and warm.
Unlike the poor ones on the outside,
They've got no 'ome where they can hide.
          No shelter from the storm.

There's some that envy me, me 'ome,
Especially when the winter comes.
          The pavement can be cold.
but I've worked 'ard to get this place,
Nobody's going to steal my space.
          This city is me world.

Martin Goldsmith Silk

BEGGAR WOMAN AND CHILD; MAJORCA

Biscuits and tea in the morning,
Dinner and coffee at night;
A bed to sleep and rest on,
In my life exists no plight.
Yet one evening I saw you
And your hand still haunts my eyes,
Oh! To see once more you
And answer your pleading cries.

When I saw you, I passed you by
Turned my face towards the sea,
Ignored the meagre outstretched hand
And the child in your arms I refused to see.

But now I sit and in my mind
Her little face, so thin, still pleads,
Now I look and soft, dark hair
On sleeping brow still falls like weeds.
Clutched in her mother's harassed arms
She curls, trusting against all harms.

And I? I passed you by,
I let you be hungry,
Perhaps even die.
I knew the score
That you knew too;
A fatherless child
So they outcast you.
It's her fault, I thought,
What care have I?

She ruined her life;
Ignore her cry.
So there sat you
And I walked by.

You begged to me and I turned away,
Oh, to return; to relive that day.

Christine Barham

THE SAME
('neath the sun)

With the same tidings
He fondles my brow
With the same givings
The gold of his plough
The stir of the soil
That is me.
That is you.
The same grain of sand.
The same sea of blue.

The shore of *my* dreams
Silent.
Bare.
My eyes, as open
My skin, as fair
The world, a stranger
With nothing to spare
But the will of the dawn
With the shake of his hair.

Carolanne Banks

CONFUSED

Once I had nice clothes, now I am dressed in rags
Once I had a suitcase, now I have got carrier bags
Once I had a good job, now I am on the dole
Once I had dignity, now I have a worried soul
Once I had a nice car, I was up there with the best
Now I have two aching legs, that need a good rest
Once I had a house, with its own little locks
Now wherever I roam, I have got a cardboard box
Once I had money, I could dine with the best
Now it's a bag of chips, with the fleas in my vest
The thing that cheers me up, through all this confuse
I am as free as a bird, I have nothing left to lose
If this world is a test, I think I read in a bible text
Then I have all my things in heaven, ready for
The next

T Allbright

THERE'S NOT ENOUGH LOVE

There's not enough love in the world today,
Which must fill some with utmost dismay.
What does it cast to be kind and understanding?
Absolutely nothing and very undemanding.
During World War Two we helped each other,
Pulling through with so little bother.
Those were terribly fearsome times,
But we all helped each other along really fine.
We were friendly respectful and sincere,
Now we are segregated living in fear,
Of reprisals and crime, with a future drear.
Why can't we respect each other more?
Whether we may be rich or poor.
Love thy neighbour, it says in the good book,
So don't be afraid to cast a look,
At each other with courtesy and care.
It would make life much easier to bear.
If only we said hello how are you?
We would all really benefit and feel so true.

Brian Watson

DES-RES

That cardboard box that you live in,
I'm sure it could be quite nice,
With some windows, and some curtains,
It could be your paradise.

You'd have a des-res of your own,
And perhaps a welcome mat,
For all to see on your threshold,
Just to see where you're whereat.

Yes that cardboard box could be nice,
With some imagination,
It could be so bright and cheerful,
And fit for habitation.

Then with an address that you have,
And the prospects you have too,
When people passed you on the street,
I'm sure they would notice you.

Peter Chaney

UNTITLED

Sitting on a wooden bench
All around an empty place
Dreaming for hours and hours
Wondering if I'll see a solemn face

The hope rises and gains power
The sight of a child on
The horizon enjoying himself
Makes my heart feel sour.

The wind approaches all
Who give in to its howl
The flowers are made to fall
The dank air is humid and foul.
No animals are seen today
They sit at home by the
Fire and cower
The rain begins to take
Its toll.
Of drenched trees roofs
And me.
Oh! How I wish I could stroll
Through a forest or by the sea.
But sadness and tears
Are all I have.
Loneliness holds the key.

Jason D Taylor

A ROLL OF THE DICE

       In a city
       there was a street
and   on that street
       there was a box
and   in the box
       there was a man
and   in the man
       there was a memory
and   in that memory
       there was a boy
and   in the boy
       there was a future
and   in that future
       there was a box.

Geoffery D Jenkins

WELCOME TO CARDBOARD CITY

No red carpet will welcome you, in our nineties cardboard city,
All dreams are long gone in lost despair, there is no sign of pity,
Find yourself a spot under a bridge, against a wall or open door,
All faces showing are gaunt and lean, it's the legacy of our poor.

Broken marriages, re-possessed homes, lost children's crying voices,
Changing circumstances forced on many people, removing any
choices,
No one purposely heads this way, it's the last stop on the line,
The fact this terminus exists at all, for this nations it's a crime.

Politicians manipulating deals in corridors of corruption and power,
Self interest and profitable ventures, deals done each passing hour,
No interest in the poor, needy and downtrodden, for them there is
no time,
Just viewed as the common masses, pass the cigars, pheasant and
port wine.

No red carpet will be rolled out for you, in our desolate cardboard
city,
All future dreams are long gone in lost despair, no sign of hope
or pity,
Many decent people are losing out, just heading for a slippery slope,
A bumpy ride on the homeless train, destination cardboard city of
no hope.

The politicians who rule our land, are not filled with friendship
or grace,
Self interest and bigoted views, with their swaggering style and
smirking face,
Fat cats in the city, sit back making personal fortunes by the score,
Feasting greedily on four course meals, wantonly ignorant of the poor.

Many people are losing their jobs, others on short time, losing
self respect,
No longer a viable proposition, for the profit gods, what can we
expect,
Many decent people are kicked out and heading for that slippery
slope,
Take care that you don't board the homeless train, destination city
of no hope.

Robert Logan

CONTRAST

Guns and roses,
Bullets and thorns.
Sweet smelling flowers
And closely clipped lawns.

Urchin by the river,
Need somewhere to sleep,
Stately home, grand with splendour,
Ten servants to keep.

Cardboard box, under the bridge,
Rats always by your side.
Duvets for a double bed,
Warmth flowing like a tide.

Sat in the street, begging for food,
There's people who'd rather not see.
They're going home to a hot square meal,
While some can't afford the taste of tea.

Julie McLennan

STREET LIFE

The pavement's dirty and all wet,
As I lay my head to sleep.
My little cardboard house is all I
have to keep.
My bedding is all dirty,
My clothes are much the same.
It's not my fault I live here, I'm
really not to blame.
No-one wants me, no-one cares,
All they do is stand and stare.
I'd love a home all warm and nice,
To have a job, to have a house,
like everybody else.
I'm not alone, I have my friends,
All much the same as me.
We share our food, our tea, our space.
Do we really belong to the human race.
You wouldn't think so, just look at my
face, it's old and lined and scared.
If only someone loved me,
And tell me they really cared.
But tonight I'm back on the pavement
Where it's all dirty and wet.
Pushed aside by shoppers, the cleaner's
broom sweeps clean.
Am I so insignificant that I cannot
be seen.
Oh Lord please help me, keep me
safe and warm
I'm sixteen, please, let me see the dawn.

Christine Regan

UNDERNEATH THE ARCHES

As the sunlight fails they make for the arches,
With cardboard for blankets and boxes for beds.
So many folk that are without homes
Shuffle along to lay down their heads
On pillows of concrete paving slabs.
What life do they lead when they live like this?
No families around them to love and hold.
How long will they survive? Do they really wish
That they were back with long lost loved ones again?
Do their families know how they are living?
And if they do, do they really care
That these once loved people are barely surviving,
Under the bridges in London town.
The odd night in a hostel and some soup from the van
May be all that they get to last for a week,
An odd copper thrown down by a sympathetic man
Passing by on his way home to his life so secure.
But maybe one day it might be this city gent,
By his family deserted and life's work complete,
That is the person, haggard and bent
That stoops to grab what is tossed his way,
As he is no longer wanted by anyone now.
All money gone and no-one will keep him,
His self respect at an all time low.
We do not know the situations
That force people to go and live on the street.
Yet we criticise without ever knowing
What in the future we are likely to meet.

Kathy Lovett

WHERE WILL I SLEEP?

Where will I sleep?
Where will I go?
I've been walking for miles,
in thick fields of snow.
I've been looking for days,
to find a safe place,
where I can sleep,
and know that I'm safe.

I saw a small shed.
Where the animals got fed.
But I'll lay on the hay,
and make it my bed.

I'll stay for a few days,
and let the snow clear.
But what is that noise?
It's just loud enough to hear.

I went outside,
to look and see.
It's a little baby reindeer,
lying on the snow,
under the tree.

Charlotte Stokes

ON RELIEF

A day comprises of many long and empty hours,
  to be filled with drudgery, toil and sweat,
  hardly a copper for a cooling draught,
  hardly a crumb left for an aching stomach.
Life on relief; some call it that.

Robin Colville

A BEGGAR'S REQUEST

Chilled to the bone
Soaked to the skin
In the damp dirty rain
I walk the streets

'Take pride' they say
'Take care' they say
But what comes of me
Tomorrow or today

Spare a pound; a coin
Throw it in my hat
You know I can't relax
Like the rich men grow fat

Give me a *bob*
Or give me a job
Give me what I need
And I will try to succeed

Gogue

STREET LIFE

Take a little trip down, to cardboard city,
Where the genre's somehow lost in meths and self-pity,
And clowns are very rare and their jokes are less witty,
Here, in this place, inner city? In a city.

This is *street life* . . . At its worst.
The underground stations are all fit to burst;
Nomadic beggars, so young, and so cursed
All lack that mother's bosom on which they were nursed;

See the cardboard cities in the cold, in the rain;
The screamers; the dreamers all going, insane;
The junkies, flunkies and their addicts, all play that game,
A *monkey* if you please, to take away that psychotic pain.

Where buskers are playing, trying to earn a bob
And hookers in abundance, twenty quid for a job;
The children; oh, the children, poor little sods,
What happened to this country, given up now, by God?

Street life . . . It ain't no longer what it used to be;
The once great adventures dreamed of, by you, by me;
Now, there's just death and degradation, beyond belief,
As we throw another copper to a jackal who never says please.

So, go ahead, take a trip, see the *street life* . . .
While children cry and men all lonely, without a wife;
And the politicians' ignorance, unbelieved, ne'er seen by their eyes,
While society ponders, complains, sticks in and twists the knife . . .

Street life . . . Certainly ain't as we would imagine,
Our ignorance towards their plight is, the ultimate sin!
On a course, a battle they, can never win;
They are poor; They are lifeless; Can I do more
As I chuck another copper into a small tin
That sits a'front a crippled man, tired, hungry, alive somehow, his
Life having been stolen from him, by what? By society's war;
Is this *street life* . . .?

Ron Matthews Jr

CLINGING ON

My heart often goes out,
To the dark shadows, which shelter in shop doorways.
Huddled, alone, litter and darkness their only companion,
Just pure luck if they wake to live another day.
Each morning relief, or maybe disappointment,
After all, their life is just one constant battle for survival.
Hungry, cold, lonely, all hope and dignity diminishing with day after
weary day,
Rummaging through dustbins for a morsel to fill their deprived
stomachs.
Others beg, only to be turned away with 'Why don't you get a job
ya lazy . . .!
They just grit their teeth and meekly continue with their gruelling
routines,
Destined for the gutter,
Too tired and weak to argue.
Just think how you and I laughed when we saw people with nowhere
to go,
Because the thought of someone not having a home was too
unrealistic,
Or how we looked upon them piteously, but couldn't bear to even
approach them.
They tolerate our ignorance because they've given up trying to
understand.
That's how they got into that state.
Ignorance, unemployment, narrow-mindedness and greed.
Why?

Kerry Pickett (14)

THE ROVING KIND

Drifting from town to town
Jobless and homeless
Footsore he wanders
Hungry he searches
A vagrant no less
A lonesome soul
I wonder what goes through his mind
Whatever is his goal
Born into this world
Just like you and me
Fought for his country
Served it gallantly
Now spurned by society
Is it by choice
Or was it by force
Made him take this course
Or was it the lack of love
Winter nights, beneath the stars
Huddled in a box
Newspaper wraps to keep him warm
Still wears his army socks
Cared for by God above
A new day dawns
He trundles on
Through spring and summer
Till the autumn has gone
Winter sees him back again
Heading for the bright lights
A shelter from the snow and rain.
One of the roving kind.

L M Dean

HARD TIMES

Some claim our country is the best
 I oftimes wonder why,
Whilst people live in a cardboard box
 and millionaires walk by.

This isn't a sign for a place that's best
 no matter what they say,
For everyone should have a home
 to live in a civilised way.

There has got to be a change in things
 to make everyone secure,
Then we can say we are the best
 when we alleviate the poor.

No one can survive on hand-outs
 they have to earn a pay,
And if homeless people get this chance
 they can throw the cardboard box away.

It is sad to see our young folk
 go begging on the street,
When all they need is a decent job
 so they can compete.

We know that in recession
 that jobs are hard to find,
But a job is their solution
 to leave the miseries behind.

Lachlan Taylor

HUNGRY MAN

Have you ever been singled out of the crowd? By a hungry man,
did you do all you can? Or did you pass him by without lending a hand?
Did you ask him if he had a secure home, or did you buy that CD you
wanted?
Did you ask him why he was hugging himself, or did you pass him by?
Tell me the truth, please don't lie,

Did you ask him why he hurts?
Or did you glance and tut?
Did you listen to his story?
Or did you find him boring?
Were you ashamed of his dirty clothes,
maybe you offered to wash them.

Oh, let's not pretend,
you passed by a,

hungry man.

David G Teahel

WINTER TRAVELLER...

It's cold dark, dismal and damp
Snowflakes are falling, no light in the lamp.
Bumper to bumper, cars in a row
Slipping and sliding on top of the snow
Icicles hang from the windows and eaves
Trees stand all naked, no covering of leaves.
People pass by, as they hurry on home
My coat's tied with string, I'm frozen to the bone.
All that I ask for is soup and a bed
Somewhere all warm, to lay down my head.
I will be gone on my way, as soon as it's light
Out of your conscience, out of your sight
But if you do see me, don't laugh whistle or sigh
Think! But for good fortune, there could go I...

T Hannah

HAVE PITY

Have pity on an old man
Whenever you pass him by,
Have pity on an old man
And let me tell you why.
The old man was a young man
Many years before,
He drank,
Danced,
And chased the girls,
He was youthful to the core.
He did all the things
That you do now,
His life was ordered and neat,
Until the day
Fate dealt a bad hand,
And he ended up on the street.
So have pity on an old man
Please listen to my plea,
Have pity on an old man,
It may turn out to be me.

James McErlean

DATE AND WALNUT CAKE

The children stood and watched him
Through the window as he walked
Up to our front door
'It's a tramp,' the youngest squawked
He asked if I would fill his flask
Perhaps give him a snack
The children watched intently
As I began to pack
Some sandwiches and fruit and then
Just as an afterthought
A slice of date and walnut cake
Home-made of course, not bought
He thanked me most politely
Then went upon his way
The children stood there quietly
And watched him in dismay
'He didn't stand a chance' they said
'He'll learn from his mistake
We won't see him again after he tastes
That date and walnut cake!'

Kim Montia

STREET PEOPLE

No home but the street
A cardboard box for a bed
Long, lonely hours of walking,
Tired, aching feet

Despised and down trodden
Moved quickly on
The traders and town folk
Wishing them gone

The seasons against them
Heavy rain and harsh winds
More often than not their food
Is the waste, salvaged from bins

Soup kitchens and charities
Provide food and clothes
Such is the dependence
Of people on the road.

Elizabeth Amery

WHEN EVIL STALKED THE STREETS

Rushing to see Argent in a Newport hall,
When out of the darkness, came the venomous call.
'How much love,' the dreadful man sneered with glee,
Heart trembling, body shaking, 'Oh God he means me.'
'You've got it wrong mate,' I turned and rallied with hate,
'I don't give my love to anyone on a plate.'
'I give my body freely to those I love and trust,'
'I don't mix with those who just want sex and lust.'
'Well you look like a whore,' came the evil reply,
'With your painted face and skirts so high,'
Keep walking, don't stop to argue with him,
If you don't play the game, his interest will dim.
Oh God! I've such a feeling of impending doom,
An evil presence hovers and looms,
Look back quickly, make sure he's far from sight,
My God a knife glinting in the cold lamplight.
What a wicked smile, such a cruel stare,
I can feel intense evil, clawing the air.
Oh run quickly! It's your one and only chance,
You could never cope with such awesome malevolence.

G E Khandelwal

OLD JIM

The people pass the cripple in the street
No one is there, no one for him to greet
His tattered clothes are all he has
Well maybe, a few things, in an old bag

He stumbles as he walks along
Through city streets and all its throng
He coughs, the phlegm nearly choking him
God bless his soul, his name is Jim

Jim finds a brazier to warm his hands
There's people like this in other lands
He takes a bite of old, stale, crust
Back to the brazier, red with rust

Then the security guard shouts at him
Is there no peace for coughing Jim
He shuffles on, head bent low
And stubs on the pavement, his little toe

He curses and damns the rest of the world
He even curses a Union Jack unfurled
Nobody cares about poor old Jim
This world, will not be long, for him

Then he makes it to the cardboard box
His unshaven face, his greasy locks
Look after him Lord, I beg you do
For Jim was once a man, solid and true.

James D Devlin

SOME CHARITY

Around the corner
they weren't quite ready
for
the tourist party.

           Then
the beggars saw
hesitated briefly
and
got set in their shoes.

           Then
they settled down
they closed up
they looked in
they looked down

           And
a wind blew
in the silent dark
moment
of charity.

           And then
they settled up
they opened up
they looked out
they looked up

           listening round.

Ray Nurse

LIFE'S RICHES

'There are times in my life when I wish I were dead'
Said the weary old man as he lifted his head.
'When I'm tired and hungry and can't find a friend,
I lay down to sleep and wish it would end,
But when I awake to the new dawn of day
The sorrows before have drifted away
And I rise from my bed made of paper and rags,
To search for my breakfast in old rubbish bags.
Some sausage, some bacon, there aren't any eggs,
A lemonade carton with just a few dregs.
A stale piece of bread will do for some toast,
From all of these scraps I must make the most.
People may turn up their nose in disgust,
But when you are hungry food is a must.
I like to be friendly with folk in the town.
Some look me up, but most put me down.
I know I'm not clean like those in a house,
And sometimes I sleep with a rat or a mouse
Who'll share my scraps and often my bed,
Or creep in my hat if it falls from my head.
All of these things help to make my life full,
For if I were like them it would become dull.
So perhaps when I think of what my life has got
I should not moan and complain of my lot.
My life is full and the riches are many
Though often I think that I don't have any.
So when I look back on the things I have said
I should not grumble, but thank God instead
For giving me freedom to live life this way,
And for giving me strength to start a new day.

Joan Rogers

HOW I FEEL - I'M HOMELESS

I'm homeless and I'm very sad
I'll never say, 'It's not so bad'
At one time I'd a lovely home
But now from place to place I roam

I'm afraid to live and afraid to die
Why did this happen to me? I sigh
The divorce it left me without a house
It belonged to the parents of my spouse

Today it is so very cold
I'm young but feel so very old
I beg for money to buy some food
I fasten my coat and put up my hood

'Go home to your parents' someone said
But mum and dad they both are dead
I am an only child you see
No brothers or sisters to help me

I wait for the toilets to open, then wash
At least they're warm and they look quite posh
I feel much better because I'm clean
Perhaps my sadness won't be seen

The people pass you by and stare
That you've no job, they really don't care
There's one thing certain that I can see
And that's an early grave for me

Janet McBride

HOMELESS AND HELPLESS

As I got off the 6:30 train,
I opened my umbrella as it started to rain.
For the occupants of Cardboard City,
I felt a hearty surge of pity.
The usual down-and-outs were there,
Together, yet alone, without a care.
Homeless and helpless, they huddled together,
Seeking protection from the inclement weather.
One man had scars and number nine shoes,
He suffered from pneumonia and smelt of booze.
As he crawled inside a battered cardboard box,
Long-nailed toes showed through the holes in his socks.
His eyes were red and his hair was thin
This poor old soul could not muster a grin.
Who knows where he'd been or where he was going,
I had no time to ask, he had no way of showing.
What past experiences had brought him to this fate?
The clock ticked on, I dared not wait.
As I threw a £1 coin into his hat,
I meandered home pensively to feed the cat.
That poor old man I will never forget,
He is loved less now than my pampered pet.
Whether once rich or hopelessly poor,
He was someone now people would just ignore.
With his deep blue eyes glazed senseless with drink,
The memory of his misery makes my heart sink.

W A Flanagan

STREET PEOPLE OF CLEVELAND

Cleveland was recently much less rich
Until various areas made a pitch
For government city challenge cash
Now smart new building work cuts a dash
An era of progress seems the rule
Is this really Stockton or Hartlepool?

Yet there is one sector
                    Where not much has changed
That hasn't been hidden or re-arranged
The street folk are there just as before
And many would say just an eyesore

But they are people and some would respond
If the powers that be could see beyond
Their outward appearance and into the need
And follow through with word and deed
Could find some pennies among the pounds
To care for these poor who are always around

Jeannette Facchini

STREET LIFE?

Have you seen him
have you seen the chap,
his eyes are glazed
his vacant stare
is dazed.
His face is old
beyond his years
his cheeks are stained
from endless tears.
His habit
all the nourishment he needs
his body
on solvents feed.
His mind
will slowly waste away
his craving
stronger every day.
He started life
as someone's child
his mother sees her son and cries.
She loved him,
loves him still
and waits,
for his return
or mourn
the day he dies.

Michael Cheney

LEICESTER SQUARE

So used to rejection
Passers-by
They don't expect anything
From anyone
Killing surprise
Greets your small gift
Your cure for guilt
Your money
Buying them time
Until the next long wait
And passers-by
On the subway stair.

A fumbled ball of humanity
Lining our streets each day
Escalating like rubbish
Disposable fast food containers
Holders devoid of anything inside
Though once they walked
Laughed and joked
With as much ease
As when you first fall in love
Reality is a shock to the system
Especially to those who dream
No streets are paved with gold
You'll have to start at rock bottom
And hope for a second
Better start
But if you fail to pass go
Just die then
Because we don't know
What to do
With any of you.

Lee Ryder

PLEASE

I did not choose to be here, although you think I did,
I ran from a cruel man, I packed and ran and ran then hid.
I thought he was the right one for me, but oh he changed so,
I could not stay and take any more, I had to finally say no.

No parents they had both passed on, no friends, nowhere to go,
I had no job, oh I wanted one, but I was now so very very low.
The state said I had to have an address to qualify for money,
the employment agent said I had also, 'He wasn't being funny.'

So here I was on the street, I wanted to work, I couldn't
I wanted a home, to be me again, help me now, no you wouldn't.
But you will all look as you pass me by, not wanting to know,
please stop hear my story, that is all you need do as you go.

What way out is there for so many of us? Who will help us?
We do not want to be here or die here, or seem to make a fuss..
So can someone change the law for us and make it one for all,
for those who often without any fault do, from society fall?

Jil Bramhall

STREET LIFE

Street life High life
Toffs off to a show
Bright light shops
Money to spend
High life Good life

Street life Low life
Live in a cardboard box
Dining out rubbish bin Wimpy
Drinking to pass the time
Low life Blurred life

Street life Animal life
High stepping poodles low slung pekes
Alley cats aristocrats
Tiny flowers between the slabs
Animal life Unnoticed life

Street life Get a life
Outside world happening daily
It's out there haven't you noticed?
See it touch it feel it smell it
Get a life Any life out there on the street

Mick Beagley

HOMELESS AND NOWHERE TO GO

I'm so far away from home
For I left and had to go alone.
I've had to survive up to now
I didn't really know how.
As my heart loses another beat
I find myself back on the street.
I walk around with my bags in hand
I find myself another night on the sand.
Weekend is once again here
The council is closed so I can't go near.
Where do I go on these cold dark nights?
For a person on the street,
Doesn't have rights.
Turned away like a big disgrace
People can't even look you in the face.
It's not my fault I have no family
I just want to live life happily.
There are no jobs to go to
Just and empty space between me and you.
Without help from people around
I spend another night sleeping on cold ground.
So spare a thought for people like me
Who have no home and had no tea.
Not all of us like to live this way
For you it's just another nice day.
One day my dream will come true
To have a nice warm home just like you.

Lynette Dunn

HOMELESSNESS

I walked along a London street
one winter's night, and saw
a city within a city.
Its buildings: cardboard carton castles,
whose princely occupants,
frost-coated,
lay curled up in
newspaper beds.
A human tragedy -
the damning disgrace of
a smug,
self-satisfied, and
self-proclaimed 'civilised'
society.

Roger Williams

CARE?

Should we care, after all we are strangers?
Should we care, we are not involved?
Should we care, it's really none of our concern?

The plea for help, looking out of sad eyes.
The hopelessness, in the voice unknown.
The huddled creature, in the doorway,
who is it, we don't know?

Stop, think, perhaps a word of encouragement
it would not go amiss, perhaps that's all that's needed
to bring it back from the abyss.

Reach out your hand and offer your assistance,
help to make him stand again.
Maybe it will be his salvation,
help the creature all forlorn.

Somewhere in the memories of childhood
are embedded things we've been taught,
don't be selfish, think of others
seems to be the common thought.

Don't be frightened, if you need help,
ask for it, it does not cost.
Advice is freely given, take it or leave it
it's at your cost.

Heidemarie Pollard

REFLECTIONS OF A SUBWAY WALL

Pass me by in haste; I surely offend your eye.
My once smooth-tiled face has aged prematurely.
I am cloaked with the lipstick, powder and paint
Of protest.

For what I see and what I feel every minute,
My stone soul screams out to reveal,
To you.

I am scratched, scribbled and sprayed on;
The graffiti of the lonely, the lost, the despairing.
Hear me.

For under the scars and disfigurement of my face,
See what I also represent to forgotten souls.
I am home.

Yes, home! They lean on me, piss on me, cry against me,
Their jumbled, forlorn heads bang on me in despair,
Every day.

I am their way, their bitter truth, their only life.
To the heads that roll against me nightly,
I am home.

They dream of walls covered with wallpaper and pictures;
Walls, with curtained windows and views.
Not a subway wall.

Bernard Curtis

KILLING TIME

Killing time.
The ultimate crime
We can commit against ourselves.
Manslaughter pleas shelved.
Each murdered second
has to be reckoned
when we stand before the bar
and take our judgement from a jar.
Waiting for sentence
terrified of penance.
For killing time
is killing life.
We accomplice ourselves
by supplying the knife.
The alley's dark.
The victim's willing.
So we pardon killing time
as a mercy killing.
Blood slickened time.
Drug quickened time.
Gliding by us on wings
so soothingly fast.
In the distance
old age gives a vicious laugh.
Raises a glass of tomorrow's dreams
and cackles a toast to crime.
Watching suicidal youth
idly killing time.

Alene Kimm

AN ALIEN THING?

Have I become quite an alien thing?
Shunned by society, I live alone
In company. At the night shelter I cling
To my identity in this home from home.

I look at the others: *dispossessed, cast down,*
Sad casualties of the New Dark Ages
- From mental hospitals closed around the town.
Something in me has died. I feel no rages.

I am so tired now - there is no point in trying,
No need, in emptiness, to keep up the pretence.
This sham of living leaves me drained, not crying.
My very existence seems to give offence.

Laura May

SUBWAY

There's 56 beds in a subway,
It's a gateway to hell at its worst.
With a cardboard city above me,
Not a penny to place in my purse.
If the economy starts going to pieces,
They'll sell it off in the land of the few.
Sending messages over their faxes,
Telling the world who they've just screwed.
The rich are feeling the bite now,
Money no longer runs free.
Now there is just one Mercedes,
Where once there used to be three.

John Kelly

THOUGHT FOR EVERY DAY

Curled up under the duvet at night
So snug, so cosy, and warm
Do we give a thought before we sleep
Of those that have no home.

For one reason or another
They are cast out on the street
Cold and hungry, tired and scared
Of undesirables they chance to meet.

Whatever it is that inspires them
Leave perhaps a comfortable home
What spurs them on to live like this
Is it the lure of the great unknown?

A cardboard box their only bed
Newspaper to cover for warmth
No feeling of warmth comes to them
Only feelings of anger and wrath.

Will it change? We hope so
To have jobs, warm clothes, warm feet
For those who return from where they came
Smiling faces are there to greet.

In an ideal world it would be so
Their dreams and aspirations we'd share
Do they really know of people like us
Give a thought that we really care.

Joyce White

STREET LIFE (IN THE OLDEN DAYS)
(Written for my six grandchildren)

You stood by a broken window
Looking down below
Watching half-clad children
Playing in Poverty Row

Who cared about their future
Or if they would survive?
They are doomed like all of us.
They had to break away or die.

What about the youngsters?
What about the shame?
What about the horrible men
Who put little children on the game?

Janet Carter

LONG HARD LIFE

When I woke up,
I had a sore head.
It must have been from,
smoking in bed.

What bed am I talking about,
I mean 'place that I sleep'.
Which is in a blanket,
On a slag heap.

Soup for breakfast . . .
and lunch and tea.
Then I check in my hat,
to see what begging's brought me.

Then maybe I'll have,
a talk with my friends.
To hope that this cruelty,
comes to an end.

Katherine Smart (12)

BIRTHDAY TREAT

I spent the night in London
It was my birthday treat
I was shocked how many homeless
Were sleeping on the streets

People were lying in cardboard boxes
The rain, it crept inside
My stomach just turned over
The tears they filled my eyes

All the properties lying empty
They could provide a home
Give shelter in the winter
Stop them freezing to the bone

An address, is what, so many need
To get themselves a job
Imagine the feeling in their hearts
As they turn their own door knob

When in your bed
Give a thought to those
Sleeping on the streets
Give a job to those who want to work
For homeless, they should not be.

Joyce Kempton

STREET LIFE

Home is where the heart is
And it needs a roof overhead
A shelter with clothing and food
Plus good night rest in a comfy bed

Some would afford a lot of luxury
And spend extravagantly
But others scrape only a necessity
Not as a miser, but just being thrifty

How could a tramp sleep on stony ground?
With all that bad weather and noisy sound
Begging for money, the old odd penny
For their stomach crying out, 'Hungry!'

Drugs, sex and violence are on the scene
They know that street life is really mean
Graffiti tell signs of their souls
Not asking for trouble but letting out their woes

Like a gypsy, travelling in a caravan
Their heart is their home
Setting up for every journey
With company or on their own.

Jenny Cheung

ONE DAY

One day I will walk with my head held high,
I won't have to cheat and I won't have to lie.
I will live in a house with a wife and a job,
no begging for me or having to rob.

One day I will drive round these streets like the Pope,
not standing in doorways wondering how I will cope.
Money in my pockets and dripping gold,
not walking around shivering cold.

One day I will be on holiday in some far-off land,
kicking my feet around in the sand.
Dining in restaurants and drinking in bars,
not lying on a bench, looking up at the stars.
So listen to my story and please hope and pray,
it's only a dream, but maybe one day.

Peter John Turner

PROBATION

Too many see.
The dog's shadow in the gutter,
Insignificant, starved by cold, limping,
Barely goes unnoticed.
Not the least tear slips unseen
Down the sleeper's face.
Stages in the passing of the night
Are fixed by stars.
If a body enters a dream
It is taken up by tongue
To be paraded later in public.
Any secretive increase
Of calm in a sensitive mind
Is registered by media
That exist by permission of fate.
The milkman knows my living
And the doctors my death.
In vain, therefore, do my steps
Seek any self-respect.
Assessments transect at street corners.
Nothing that has dared to exist
But has been weighed, judged, found wanting.
The insolent, uncaring world
In its most insidious guise -
Lover, brother or boss -
Cuts all down to size.
Small wonder so many suffer
A general paralysis of the inane.
The scrutiny is uncompromising,
The diagnosis direct.

Alasdair Aston

NOT WORTH A LABEL

Brain dead
Underneath
The baseball
Caps . . . !
Reversed to hide
Some fears
From peers,
And like style
Morons,
All entrapped
With sweaty
Feet,
In ninety nine quid
Pumps
Strutting stuff
In uniforms,
Alike . . .
Can't read, can't think,
Can't talk, can't write,
Save marking *X*
On Giro cheques!
Dependent, in the
Underclass
Of shame!

Wm Paul McDermott

THE FORGOTTEN ONES

Whoever I am, and wherever you find me, I'm not alone,
somewhere in the unfriendly outdoors, where I roam,
always hungry, and usually cold, that's me and my kind,
what will be my home today? Whatever I can easily find,
a doorway, or a park bench maybe, hopefully dry and warm,
we the invisible ones, in our clothes tattered and torn,
on concrete and grass we all sleep, in search of food,
understand our aimless lives, and our impenetrable moods,
misery is all we have in us, without a home to live in,
you have a roof over your head, I have none, for all my sins,
where shall I huddle up tonight? In my old shoes and socks,
perhaps in some bushes, or maybe if I'm lucky, in a cardboard box,
yes, we may have loved ones, but they don't know or care,
save us with our dignity, from all this crushing despair.

Christopher Higgins

STREET LIFE

'Trouble,' Mum shouted at me.
'Thanks for being so understanding.'
The comfort of a roof over my head,
The food on the table to warm me
on a cold winter's night,
a warm bed to sleep in,
gone, with a few words spoken on
the spur of the moment.

Cold winter nights, cold to the bone,
no hot food to warm me up
no warm bed to sleep in
only a cold doorway, huddled, shaking, sobbing.
'God, I look awful.'
I was once so tidy, smart even in my
new suit I bought for an interview,
but, look at me . . .
I can't go back, I just can't
not after the way Mum treated me . . .
I just can't.

My life will be like this forever,
I don't know what to do,
one voice says *Stay*, one voice says *Go*,
I see a young woman, looking old, a real mess,
shock, sadness, horror, it scared me.
Do I have the courage to return?
I had enough courage to leave.
Knock, knock, 'Hello Mum, it's me, I'm home.'

Nia Smith

NO LIFE

Homeless desperation,
Head against the wall.

Financial commitment,
Wallstreet fall.

Personal dignity,
Nothing left.

Clothes in tatters,
Turn to the meths.

Future plans,
Are nowhere to be found.

Family figures,
Move without sound.

Morals and pride,
Don't make me cry.

Drugs and alcohol,
Life's only high.

Food and water,
My daily war.

Past experiences,
Have made my life sore.

Debra Neale

LIFE ON THE STREET

I cannot think how life must be with no-one ever wanting me
No warmth no love oh God above why does this have to be?
I'm living in a cardboard box I've had enough of life's hard knocks
I'm cold I'm destitute I'm poor I'm sorry if it shocks

When people pass me sweet and clean I think of how life could have been
But nowadays there's no compassion this is clearly seen
My bleeding heart is torn and sore on me the world has closed its door
I'm living in life's litter bin that's all there is in store.

I wonder where the problem lies, it lies in broken family ties
Rejected by one's kith and kin oh can't you hear their cries?
Solutions we should try to find, perhaps if we were less unkind
I know there is no easy way but let's not be too blind.

It's easier to just ignore the plight of thousands who are poor
The shunned unwanted castaways, the jetsam on life's shore
But there but for the grace of God it could perhaps be me
So let us strive to clear the streets of all this poverty.

Barbara Hampson

LIVING DEAD

I am the Outer Shell
as I walk through the Vacuum of Life:
I sleep in a cardboard box,
I eat from bins
and wear plastic bags as socks:
I no longer pluck my eyebrows,
I no longer shave,
I long for a bath
but the financial cost
would put me in the grave.

T E Nolan

STREET LIFE

I'm forming a mind of my own
Working out the seeds I've sown
Most nights I move with the crowd
Cruisin' the streets of this town
But sometimes I drop the heat
Ignore the beat of the street
Gotta work my head into place
Figure out why it's such a waste

Street life - the only game to play
The message is sold all the way

Time after time it's the same
Feel I'm trapped inside this game
Nothin' changes much at all
Boredom pins me against the wall
But sometimes I turn my back
Decide not to run with the pack
Escape from the street's bad news
Walk the way I want to choose

Street life - the only way to be
But fantasy don't come for free

Drowning inside the crowd
Somethin' inside screams out loud
Why do I float with the pack?
My life has got to be -
Better than that . . .

Street life takes you down below
Strips away your heart and soul

Street life gets inside your head
Leaves the truth of you for dead

Bernard Harry Reay

THE TRAMP

His tatty clothes are ripped and torn,
He searches every street,
Inside the town where he was born,
To find a scrap to eat,
He sorts through rubbish thrown away,
It's all that he can do,
He lives his life from day to day,
But not like me and you,
He doesn't get a daily meal,
He hasn't got a home,
It's hard to know how he must feel,
Being all alone,
Then when daylight turns to dark,
It's time for him to go,
He finds a bench inside the park,
And prays it doesn't snow,
He wraps his coat around him tight,
To try to beat the cold,
And wonders if he'll be alright,
He knows he's growing old,
He dreams of things that he has done,
In this old life of his,
But knows he's not the only one,
Who has to live like this.

Carolyn Finch

STREET LIFE

Suddenly I awake,
A sharp pain in my back,
They want me to move on.

Was I dreaming?
So I'm still here,
Roaming the streets,
Nowhere to go.

What lays in store for me today?
Maybe I'll visit the park,
Watch the birds eat.

What shelter will I have tonight?
The park bench,
A cardboard box?

There's no room,
At the shelter,
No hot food,
No place to rest my head,
No room at the inn,
I know how they felt now!

Entrapped,
No fixed address,
No job,
So no benefits,
Even if I wanted to escape the street life!

Kim Rands

CARDBOARD DREAM

Through a hole in my cardboard box
I watched the leaves falling
From the sycamore trees
As they floated to the ground
Landing on the grass beneath
As softly as a whisper

A carpet was forming
From nature's mellow riches
Yellow, gold and brown
Warm and inviting
Gently beaconing the autumn
To awaken to its harvest

People walked by
Ignoring the beauty
And cursing the children
For wading through the crispness
And getting dust on their shoes
But I saw perfect art revealed:

Intermingled with the leaves
Were 'bus tickets, sweetie papers
And cigarette packets
Scattered with random
Yet, like a famous masterpiece
In tasteful array

Cellophane and silver foil
Glittered like a galaxy of stars
Or fairy lights on a Christmas tree
And the artist's signature
Propped against the shop doorway
Was an empty lager can

Lilian Conway

STREET PEOPLE

I've put on your shoes, left mine behind
To try to see what I can find,
It's cold, it's dark, my bones are aching
The pain is real - there's no mistaking

I try to fathom what I would do
If you were me and I were you
I feel guilty, I feel shame
I ask myself who's to blame

The plight of such people is a sad affair
Filling me with unease - with despair
If I came from a different home
It could be me there, all alone

Home again, I put on my shoes
The other pair I am happy to lose
One thing I have learnt from my trip
Is that society today is very sick

Gladys C'Ailceta

EVENING RUSH HOUR

laying alone in the bleak subway
a hibernating animal
under winter cover
merged with shadows
an unmoving lump
slumped on the ground - forgotten
there to be stepped over
briefly glanced at
quickly passed by

not warm, but cold
not dry, but wet
not well, but ill
not cared for
to be commented on
like a fact of life
an image for the rest of us
of someone else's problem

Michael Bell

ALONE ON THE STREET

I live on the street
The next doorway I find
Is where I'll sleep.
I wake in the morning
All stiff and cold
To a giant policeman
Standing so bold
I creep away in the rain
My body is aching
And I'm in pain
It's not the way I want it to be
I thought it was great
To leave home and be free
No-one telling me what to do
Or shouting, get out of that bed
Lazy lump you
Now all I've got
Is a cardboard box
And a great big hole
In one of my socks
I didn't realise the money wouldn't last forever
And now I've ended up being a beggar
How will it end?
What will I do?
My thoughts are all muddles
To think it all through
My life's in a mess
I've nowhere to go
But to walk the streets
And feel all alone.

Joy Willoughby

SIGNPOST

Sometimes the signpost isn't very clear
And eyes are blinkered when in fear -
A rainy night - runaway, not old -
Signs of desperation and feeling cold.
Stealthily walking down leafy lane -
Darkness - yet a light from a window-pane.
To get away from home is the only thing.
To get away from hurt - life's bitter sting.

Sometimes the signpost isn't very clear -
Rubbing hand to hide a tear -
Glad to get away from family mob,
Going to find a place and a bright new job.
Feeling hungry - I'll make a dash -
Driver stopping - that's just great -
Won't let on I'm in a state.

Sometimes the signpost isn't very clear -
And Oh! If only love were near,
The traffic lights - then a pull-in place,
I mumble 'Thanks' - a smile for face.
People looming and traffic fast -
Lights are burning - shadows cast -
Noise - confusion - where to go?
Shops all standing in a row.

Sometimes the signpost isn't very clear -
That's why I've just landed here.
The doorway's big and will do tonight -
Tomorrow begins the onward fight
To search for love, for job and home -
To settle down - no more to roam.

Pat Melbourn

TIME TO GO

Sitting all alone, I start to doubt,
What life is really all about.

Beautiful is the world to live in,
But the people how they sin.

They rob and steal for fun at times,
God will pay them for their crimes.

How I long for my time to come
To visit that paradise in the sun.

I pray for this they call the living,
People are not prepared for giving.

My time is near I hope and pray,
To find myself in the other land one day.

Peace on earth, just not so,
I pray it's my time to go.

I lie in wait and wonder why,
Nobody seeks me from that land in the sky.

Oh please, oh please, you must come soon,
How I hate this lonely, lonely room.

It's colours all around me so,
Oh please, oh please, it must be my time to go.

Diana Chaplin

IT'S THE WAY ME MUVVER PUT ME 'AT ON . . .

I ain't got no brains, 'cos I bunked offa school
an' spent all me time in the bars playing pool
but that got real borin', so went into crime -
the money ain't bad and it passes the time

I'd like to get shacked up and knock out some kids
but way fings are goin', me life's on the skids
when I was a nipper, I dreamt I'd get rich
by being hot stuff on Millwall's football pitch

Me 'scuses for muggin' may seem a bit lame
but old man's in nick and me mum's on the game
me sister's a junkie and bruv's on the booze -
the way that I see it, I've nuffin to lose . . .

Sue Millward

UNDER THE ARCHES

Under the arches, there's a cardboard city,
where recycling a life, more than just green,
beds from boxes with sheets of newspaper.
Under the arches, beneath a roof of pity,
too open for warmth, far too high to clean,
not that cleanliness is part of this caper.

Under the arches, centre of life on the street,
for the homeless, the drifter, the runaway,
the mugger, the unfortunate, the drug taker.
Under the arches, checked by Old Bill's beat,
a soup kitchen priest offers a chance to pray,
a place forgotten by politics society maker.

Les Merton

CARDBOARD HOUSES

It's raining
Again -
Acid rain,
Merging with
Salty rivulets
On our rosy,
Cold bitten
Skin;
Trying to
Get in
To our souls
And wash
Away
Our last traces
Of
Hope -
And
Our cardboard houses
Turn to
Pulp.

Christine McNaught

CARDBOARD CITY

Cardboard city!
It's not very pretty.
Cardboard homes, all in a row.
Full of hopeless people
with nowhere else to go.

Cardboard city!
It's not very pretty.
At night, it's damp and cold.
Bad enough if you are young.
A killer if you're old.

Cardboard city!
It's not very pretty.
Who is there to blame?
Blame the tramps, the nobodies.
They didn't play our game.

Cardboard city.
It's not very pretty.
It's ugly but it's there!
It's part of our community.
And community should care.

Ann Anderson

FIGURES AT A FIRE

Flame lights their faces
As they hug the heat.
The woman gaunt, graceless,
Legs apart.
Three men slouching, swaying,
Shadowy in the dusk.
Life in a bottle passes
Hand to hand,
Mouth to mouth.
Smoke rises, fades, vanishes.
Like hope unrealised.

John McKibbin

STREETS OF BRAZIL

Children being killed on the streets of Brazil.
Orphans, neglected, lonely, dirty.
Policemen are shooting these young souls.
Being paid by businessmen,
Street kids steal to stay alive
The misery these souls have to bare.
Daily hunger and any food they have to share.
Dirty clothes snotty faces grime ingrained bodies
No hope or ease.
Whatever they do or say they just can't please.
The pavement being their home.
Who are they? Identity unknown.
Unable to trust no-one cares.
They are sons and daughters of mothers and fathers.
Human rights and all that crap.
Police guns are fired to kill the young.
Abuse from adults must end, does anyone help
To convict the guilty?
Living a lonely life on the streets with crowds,
Traffic, noise, and squalor.
Drugs, abuse from others so close at hand.
Some depend on sex and one-night stands.
Young boys and girls becoming prostitutes just hoping.
No shine in their eyes dreading each day
They need safe shelters and hope to know the way.
Away from crime not having to steal to survive,
Who will give them a caring smile.

Beaney Hall-Quibell

THE 'LADY' OF THE NIGHT

Her childish figure and her soft trusting eyes
Are hidden by make-up and the punter's harsh cries.
Her pimp 'does the business' organising the man.
While she gets 'it' over with as fast as she can.
Then back to her bedsit and a few shameful tears
How long can she take this - for how many more years?

All to be happy - to be a child one day
That was her dream - the reason why she ran away.
Away to the street - lights that seemed safer than home
Away to the city where she'd 'go it alone'.
But she's trapped now again by her fears and in fright
With no-one to turn to, the 'lady' of the night.

Lynsey Whitmore

THE STREET MARKET

The sound of a street market fell on our ears.
We ran down the kerb in our haste.
A crowd packed the roadway and as we approached
We found it was just to our taste.

The stallholders harangued the mob as they tried
To sell all their stock in a day.
'Come on, ma, give 50 pence, 45 then,
At 40 I give it away.'

Folk jostled each other all trying to get
To stalls to buy bargains galore.
They spent all their money and tried to decide
Whether they should go home and get more.

Collectors were there - they were smart and well-dressed -
They wanted old prints and antiques.
The dealers were hoping to sell for £5
What just cost them tenpence most weeks.

The jugglers and acrobats all plied their trades.
Balloon sellers passed with their wares.
The people were watching in holiday mood.
Forgotten were problems and cares.

A strain on a saxophone drifted our way.
Its sound little more than a sigh.
The hauntingly beautiful tone filled the air
And rose like a breath to the sky.

As we strolled through the crowds we observed more and more
Empty boxes piled up on the ground.
The stallholders started to take down their stalls,
Then went on their way homeward bound.

Joyce M Turner

MISERY MAN

I'm walking down the street one day,
Happy as can be,
When I come across a lonesome man,
Resting on one knee,

I ask him what's the matter,
And he looks into my eyes,
His mud-stained face cries for help,
Its features old yet wise,

He reaches out for my hand,
His hands are old but worn,
And as I take it helpfully,
I see his clothes are torn,

His bristly beard brushes my skin,
And his paper bag hits the floor,
The smell of alcohol fills the air,
And I won't help him anymore,

I let go of his hand and walk away,
Angry that I cared,
And he shouted at me for spare change,
And the peak of my anger flared,

For the reality was hidden from me,
In an old and unhappy face,
For the innocent to stumble upon,
The truth in his embrace.

Claire Piwawarski (16)

CROSSROADS

I've reached this certain stage in life,
When I still don't know what I want to do,
I know that I shouldn't carry on this way,
Because aimlessness is a disease so blue,

But I've always drifted from job to job,
Usually taking the first good offer to come,
Although now I've been made redundant,
It feels as if I'm unwanted by some,

You could say that I've reached the cross-roads,
Not just in work but in life as well,
For an opportunity I should seize,
The chance to rise up out of hell,

Now I know that this story has a moral,
And its message is there for all to see,
Get up young man and stir yourself,
Because nothing in life is really free.

Myke Duncan

URBAN REJECTION

You can keep your urban life and underground line
The hustle and bustle, appointments on time
The stale polluted air
Drug pushers who don't care
Putting others into a life of crime

The army of homeless on the streets at night
In cardboard boxes can't be right
At home your wife
This stressful way of life
Makes you wonder of your children's plight

Up north in the isles, the way of life for me
Where the air is fresh from the sea
No violence, no crime rate
No drug problem to-date
Yet: Why do 10 million Londoners disagree?

Harrold Herdman

LIFE'S TOO SHORT CLARE

Life's too short to be jealous
Because there's people better than us,
Life's too short to cry
When luck passes you by,
Life's too short to worry
About intelligence, looks and money,
Life's too short to moan
If life feels too much, you're not alone,
Life's too short to give up, keep fighting
Make the lonely days exciting,
Life's too short to forget to care
About the less fortunate ones everywhere,
Life's too short to feel sorry for yourself
Even if you're not in the best of health,
Life's too short to be someone you're not
Just make the most of what you've got,
Life's too short to say that's not fair
That's life, so don't despair,
Life's too short to dwell in the past
With bad memories that wanted to last.

Come home I want you back.

Karen Cook

LIVED IN SMELL

Sad grey eyes with lived in smell
Scan the world from a cardboard box.
Begging for love, hoping for food
Seeing judgements darting his way and peering over walls to make
their decision.
Too slack trousers, too lean body, too many memories.
Plastic bag world offers its comfort
Offers finality, offers fantasy.
Is he a prince or only a pauper, incognito lover
Of some high born lady.
A product of greed? Abandoned baby?
Or haunted and hunted like an animal with rabies.
Sad grey eyes crusted on dirt
Shoes held together with thick 'lastic bands
Sleeps under bridges welfare is twilight
Sex is forgotten
Damp, wet and sodden . . . But never down-trodden
A model of peace and poise and composure.
Feared by the children, side stepped by old ladies
The unenviable stench is his calling card
Frozen in winter, rancid in summer, but please remember
He's some mother's son.
Sad grey eyes with a story to tell
A history, a life, he's hidden so well.

Frances McFaul

THE WINDFALL

It was twenty past three in the morning,
And shuffling up Palmerston Place
In a fine chilling rain, came a vagrant
With hopelessness writ on his face.

Up his shirt was last Wednesday's *Scotsman,*
Round his seat wound the *Evening News,*
And someone's discarded *Big Issue*
Plugged the gaps in his leaky old shoes.

A screeching of tyres drew attention
To a van with a dubious load;
As it sped past, the back door flew open
And a carton fell into the road.

Without the delay of a second,
The vagrant, a gleam in his eyes,
Lugged the carton down Grosvenor Crescent
For a leisurely look at his prize.

Inside was a massive computer,
A wonder he'd ne'er before seen,
And he pondered awhile in the drizzle
Which bespattered the monitor screen.

O what joy filled the heart at that moment
Of this soul used to naught but hard knocks!
The computer was left on the pavement,
And the vagrant made off with the box.

Ken Angus

UP FROM THE STREETS

I know the pavement through the soles of my feet
As I trudge the long dark trench, the city streets.

You see, I'm in a rut so deep
I can hardly see over the edge.

Stan Downing

THE HURDY GURDY MAN

In a sheltered doorway of an opulent bank,
he rests his weary body, the ageing,
smiling, Hurdy Gurdy Man.

Impatient shoppers, bleary eyed from domestic
worries, *puddlejump* on a wet November
morning and ignore silent monetary
pleas of the ageing,
smiling Hurdy Gurdy Man.

The mendicant reject, with low spirit and
aching arm delivers discordant tunes
that jingle like a cat's concert,
still he smiles,
the ageing, smiling Hurdy Gurdy Man.

Like his life, his coat is full of holes
revealing tarnished medals of a valiant
hero, who became the
ageing, smiling Hurdy Gurdy Man.

A Branthwaite

THE TRAMP

He sits, what does he see?
His face a mask,
Eyes that look out on the world but do not see,
A shaggy beard, long hair
A face so worn and tired
A shabby coat worn with time
Trousers shiny from wear.
A black bin liner to hold his belongings
A sad face that sees not the people passing by,
But some inner thoughts not for the world to know,
Of things long held in his memory
Of times past of loves lost
Of friends perhaps long gone
People walk past him
Some stare, some show no interest
He may be some bundle of baggage
Or just a jumble of old clothes
He doesn't mind, doesn't even seem to notice,
Lost in his own thoughts
Lost to the world long gone from him
Children sometimes mock him
Or just stand and stare, from young eyes that do not understand
He may be wise for all they know
With wisdom beyond their years.
His home is now the streets
His bed a bench or doorway
He lies huddled in his old clothes
No blanket to cover him no pillow for his head.
For this is his home.

Hazel Webb

THE BASHERS' NIGHT OUT

The bashers cough and shiver in hovels so dank
As royalty steps out from a taxi rank.
She never reflects on her obscene wealth
While the bashers all curse their worsening health.
The new lad appeared some days ago
His eyes soon lost their happy glow
We suspect he has reason to live as we do
Redundant skills are the usual clue
Such a waste of our generations
Another failure for their job creations.
Old Joe - how he struggled with coldness and blues
Eking out existence in his worn-out shoes
He finally succumbed, an ambulance took him away
If he'd seen all the fuss it would have made his day.
Tonight as you slide between warm cotton sheets
Think of the bashers on dark city streets
Forgotten generations we all ignore
Who are glad to sleep on a cold concrete floor.

Jim Averill

CARDBOARD CITY

What's happened to Britain? Our good land,
Where people once were so proud to stand,
It's gone to the dogs, it's looking grim,
Gaunt-looking faces, homeless and slim,
Our big cities, just walk them at night,
Men, women and children, heartbreaking sight,
No homes for them can anyone find,
People walk past as if they're blind,
They sleep in boxes just on the ground,
Beg on the streets, no money around,
The adults can't work, they are too old,
Children too young, or so I am told,
So many reasons why they are there,
Who gives a damn? Help or wants to care,
All I can say, it is a pity,
People live in a cardboard city.

Ann Dulon

HOMELESSNESS

H omelessness happened to my sister, Anne;
O ne day a home, husband, dog and van,
      - then
M idday the next, the bailiffs arrived
      - and
E verything they owned was thrown outside.
      - For her
L ife had been secure and a laugh,
      - with
E *venings* often spent luxuriating in a bath.
      - Now
S he had to sleep on the beach, under stars,
      - existing
S crimping and scraping - even washing cans.
N ever did she dream her life could be,
      - one
E ndless round of poverty.
S treet life was her way for several years,
      - until
S SAFA put an end to all her fears.

Elaine Duggan

OUTDOOR IS INDOOR

A love for life
which no-one can see,
sleeps in the park under
the chestnut tree,

A poor life but with
wealthy sense,
having a pound in the hand is
knowing less than having pence,

Drunk on a harmonica deep
down in the subways,
songs played ;in chapped lips
and fingertips in mitten frays,

One with the world
sky's the roof of home,
people are the television and
birds are the telephone.

Natasha Baker

T-JUNCTION

Standing still
Passers-by
All a blur
Babies cry
One hundred mile
A thousand years
Standing here
Close to tears
Rushing past
Pushing by
It's so fast
I will die
Spinning top
Round and round
Never stop
Makes no sound
Noiseless people
Have no say
Looking on
Just in the way.

Russell J Poynter

STREET LIFE

Where am I going, no people for knowing
As I wander and wander,
Go toing and froing.
A lonely, tired person in a land of no friendship.
Just spending what life's left
In a cardboard compartment.

I see all these bottles which lie with the others.
Watch old and the young ones
That I call my brothers.
Such lonely, tired people in a land of no friendship.
Just shaking and trembling in a cardboard compartment.

Each day as I squander the pittance
I beg for.
But nobody gives much, I suppose you can't blame them,
'Cos they're not lonely, tired people
In a land of no friendship,
Or living their lives in a cardboard compartment.

Jackie Hyde

THE SLEEPING BAG

I roll the bags and try to get a hold that
they will go into the fabric cover bag.
'Should I spend the night under the stars
in this bag the morning I'd never see.'
Train my tummy to go without my tea, supper
and so on.
Now the clock has taken a backward turn,
the weather has caught on fast, chilling
the bone and the heart.
Thousand jobs on the go each day fewer
roofs to cover our heads.
'Tis now it's getting to our ears and some are a
little concerned as soon this could happen
to us too and it is now real when it's getting
near the fear.

Margaret Gleeson Spanos

UNDESIRABLE

To say I roam
Without a home
Because I fear real life
And that I shirk
The stress of work
And mortgage, kids and wife
Suggests that 'real'
Means never feeling
Doubt as to your worth
And that your needs
And mouths to feed
Will justify your birth

But hang on a minute . . .

You've found your ways
To fill your days
And leave no room for thought
To love yourselves
And line your shelves
With things that you have bought
You've learned the drills
And social skills
And bourgeois shibboleths
You dim your lights
With Diamond Whites
To simulate your deaths

And you say *I* can't handle reality?

The Adjuster

TO EACH HIS OWN

Are they just a special breed
  A pasteboard box,
    A drink, a 'weed'
Hail, rain, snow, in any weather
  Some nearly in the
    'Altogether'

A house and home
  For all too many
Barely exist
  Can't spare a penny
Perhaps like in the animal world
  This is how our lives unfurled
Some caged, and fed
  'Makes do and mends'
Others look to,
  Their 'own ends'

'Hobson's'
  To a fair degree
The pavement, box,
  Or council key
Lord in His image
  Maketh man
The winner, second,
  'Also ran'

Liam McKinney

UNTITLED

The girl with the bombshell eyes
        stares at the rain
fragmented
        distorted
                she is a raindrop
contact
        water/stone
she understand the force of splinters

        her eyes
                split up and spattered
dissolve the light

Sophie Levy

STREET LIFE

Living in a box.
Every day. Poorer and poorer
in every way. No home
to go to. No food to
eat because that's the
way I'm living on
the street. The government
need to take note
should all get together
and have a vote.
Please give them a
comfy bed, instead of
seeing them on the
streets may be dead.

Charlotte Bibb (12)

GOLDEN SMILE

Girl sat on the pavement
looking so sad and cold
you sit there so meekly
so silent and still
your hat small and empty
with so few shining coins
hungry and homeless
says your little sign.
Your lot I would not wish
on a daughter of mine
this mile may be golden
but it doesn't look so for you
the crowds they all push by
they all look so well fed
they'll drive home in warm cars
to their nice cosy bed.
The money so wasted
on the cheap tacky gifts
may keep you from hunger
or find you a bed.
If each father among them
left a few little coins
this mile would be golden
and maybe then we'd see
your own golden smile.

Terence I Rush-Morgan

LIFE ON THE STREETS

I've lived on the streets for a year now,
It's a really hard life out there,
Each day is spent on road corners,
Asking, 'Have you any money to spare?'

Night-time is what I really fear,
I'm too scared to rest my head,
I never know if I'll see the morning,
If I'll be alive or - I could be dead.

I've been told I should go back home,
But I know it'd be no use,
With only my stepfather living,
And the painful memories of abuse.

My home is a cardboard box,
The food I eat isn't great,
I wish I had a real family,
My life is one I've grown to hate.

Rachel Collier (15)

IT'S HELL ON THE STREETS

For me no nice warm bed,
The pavement is where I lay my head,
Sometimes I feel that I would be better off dead,
I am young but look so old,
It's living with the elements,
You know the lashing rain the winter's cold.

I am tired and ill fed,
Begging for a single slice of bread,
No family life for me, not even a hot cup of tea,
For me a simple cardboard box,
No front door or safety of the locks.

And am I free? No! Not me,
There's danger all around,
My heart jumps in the night at every tiny sound,
I pray that soon I'll find a humble room,
Where I can have a nice warm bed,
A pillow on which to lay my head.

If I could have my dream come true,
I'd want a home, and it's the truth I am telling you,
It's hell on earth out on the streets,
No comfort, no family, no happy laughter,
I am not asking for the moon,
Oh it's just a home I am after.

Terri Brant

CARDBOARD CITY BLUES

We wake up in the morning, aching, cold as sin,
if a doctor examined us, where would he begin?
We've got hepatitis, impetigo and TB.
We've got staphylococcus, head lice and fleas.
So we stagger across the pavement to beg from you please.

We've got the cardboard city blues, if we had a job tomorrow
this wouldn't be the life we'd choose.

We wake up in a doorway in the middle of the night,
a drunken dosser's kicking us and asking for a fight.
We've been rolled for our money, our shoes and our beds,
we're tired, cold and hungry,
what can we do, but beg?

We've got the cardboard city blues, if we had a job tomorrow
this wouldn't be the life we'd choose.

All we want is some food, a place to lay our heads.
A bath when we're dirty,
when it's cold a soft warm bed.
But no one seems to care what a state we're in.
We were born losers, never seem to win.

We've got the cardboard city blues, if we had a job tomorrow
this wouldn't be the life we'd choose.

Doreen Russell

A PROUD BEGGAR IN OLD LONDON

'Cuse me, fine gentlemen,
where are the pretty ladies then,
in their fine, feathery hats -
still in your crumpled beds?
Give me money, money -
round, shining and thin,
but not made from tin!
The ones I adore are old,
made from pure gold.
Kindly let me see it then
in your elegant hand.
'Beg your pardon - no?
Well, off you go
with yer money, a curse of Man!
Why, 'twas not even worn
in a leather purse
when you were born!
Money - pah, stand aside 'sar',
and let me pass - a beggar.'

Etelka Marcel

A POUND A ROUND

'Big Issue' 'Help the homeless'
Decrepit life, the cry so worthless
A thousand eyes, sightless and numb
Watch for a winter, the cold will come.

Doorways are my bedsits again for the night.
Poor chap, bad luck, oh what a sight.
A dream pushes in, with a smile on my face
I recall my childhood, the whole human race.

I can still be happy, I can still be me.
I can be myself, I can live it free.
Cold I'm so cold, please give me a life,
Before it ends, on the point of a knife.

It's dangerous without family and friends
There's drugs, and booze, a means to an end.
Don't blame me because I have no home,
I've tried to explain in this poem.

How it feels alone at night in the snow.
Feet swelling up. Do you really know,
Your mind plays tricks in such a state,
Now it's times like this you need a mate.

No-one wants to live this way.
It's how you feel and what you say.
No-one respects a tramp with cold eyes
And newspapers don't care with all their lies.
Awake again my bones cold and stiff.

A O'Donovan

STREET SONG (A CHRISTMAS CAROL)

'Away in a manger,
Nor crib for a bed'
I haven't a pillow
To rest my poor head;
Nobody cares if
I lie here and die,
The world is my home,
And my roof is the sky;
The elements toss me
From pillar to post,
But uncaring people,
They hurt me the most;
Because I am shabby,
My clothes are unkempt,
They treat me with scorn,
With their looks of contempt;
They know not the reasons,
They know not my sorrow,
I've suffered today,
And I'm dreading tomorrow;
As they rush on their way,
And turn a blind eye,
Nobody cares if
I live or I die;
'Away in a manger,
No crib for a bed'
I hope by tomorrow,
That I will be dead.

Dorothy Neil

WALKING IN A WINTER WONDERLAND

The service is a little slow, they're running out of ice,
By winter in the Maldives, chaps, is really rather nice;
My cardboard box is broken, oh for a mug of tea!
This winter under London Bridge will be the death of me.

We love All Hallows parties, the apples bob like corks,
Please Mummy can Jemima stay? Look Daddy it's Guy Fawkes;
A burger if you're lucky, and perhaps a lemonade,
Then back down to that Refuge place that's run by Women's Aid.

I'm whizzing down the Alpine slopes, my speed is supersonic,
And après -ski is better still, with double gin and tonic;
I'm dashing down the Welfare, 'cos my Giro's overdue,
The snow is thick, my T-shirt's thin, I think I've got the flu

We're on survival training, we're canoeing down in Poole,
We're outward bound, we're all dressed up, we come from public
school;
My hands are numb, my feet are wet, I'm bloody sick of yelling
Big holes in jeans, big holes in socks, Big Issue isn't selling.

The trouble with a winter cruise - decisions all the time,
The deck, or pool, or hair saloon, or lemon juice or lime;
The trouble if you're old and poor, the choices are so hard,
Turn up the heat, or pay the rent, or buy some marge or lard.

In plush and cosy offices of ministers of state,
The end of session revelry is going on till late,
But in gloomy home and refuge, on the street, and under arch,
The winter of our discontent - an army on the march!

Peter Davies

A MATTER OF CHANCE

He gained his spurs on the seaside piers,
Ten pence a go with a choice of machines,
And the coins jangling flow,
Left his eyes all aglow.

'Twas no big deal but he enjoyed the thrill,
Of the tumbling coins spewing into the tray,
Giving good choice of play for just one more day.

The days grew longer and school was forgotten,
Evening beckoned, made its dark, chilling call,
The urge became stronger but the coins fell far fewer,
Machines were now deafening, more clever and newer.

You'll rue these bad days his teachers pleaded,
For a good education will ensure a bright future,
And even his parents regretted the day
They showed him the pier and gave him his way,
For learning by practice is not the best tutor.

At last he was free and schooldays were over,
No A level passes but he was in clover
So off to the pier, no more playing truant,
His luck would be in he'd be quite affluent.

He had soon left his family (thrown out far more likely)
Lived in a squat, tried begging went hungry,
For handouts don't pay well, they rarely advance,
But still in his mind he was in with a chance.

Then came the big day when he just knew he'd make it,
The pound was saved up and no-one could take it,
One lottery ticket and his dreams were not shattered,
For the numbers he'd chosen they had really mattered.Who needs the A
levels or a first class degree?

They're still out of work, take one look at me,
A swanky Porsche car and a mansion to live in,
Some months in Las Vegas and fine destinations,
For timely good luck is the real education.

Edgar Wall

BUS SHELTER

At night in a bus shelter it is dark
With only voices to stand next to
Dark
Voices and the shadowed trail they leave.
Sad that he felt so little he prayed the bus would come.
The tattoo, wallowing in an impatience
One over the eight made,
Kept bumping, knocking and thumping
With breeze-block fists
As the sweat on the windows
Bore tribute to an artist
Soz woz ere B4U
And grinned, paneless, like an old mouth
Dark.
Tempers rose as bladders stretched
And no-one really cared to bet
That the leatherette youth
Would continue to queue
When the bus pulled up.

Christopher Straker

THE BEGGAR

This man's in the gutter. Don't understand why
Because we've just gone on, and reached the sky
He's seen the world, crash around him somehow.
The mask is in place, as we pass by
How could he sink so low on the ground?
When we have our yacht, pavilions, and mound.
Of wealth overflowing, our position is sound
Hesitate, and remember, it's so easy to fall
From grace and character, besmirched, derided
His face shows it all
So whenever we see the beggar, so small
With tin box and monkey, invisible there
Dragging him lower, beneath our feet
Remember bad judgement, derision, are waiting to snare
You and me, as that beggar cries out to the Lord
'Why is it I've sunk down? Please give me a word'
Kindness, compassion, he needs your assistance
To rise above his station, with resistance
Remember this path, is only a small distance

Albert Boddison

SUNDAYS IN SCUNTHORPE

Where curtains don't quite meet, pale dawn
Light arrives, and stencils cool grey
Window-shapes on opposite walls
Indoors. Midland Sundays scorn
Anyone who'd keep them at bay.
Heedlessly, the sunshine calls

Exuberant pups out for walks
In tree-lined parks, Central, Quibell -
Redolent with muzzle-worthy
Joys, inspiring inter-dog talks.
Tails thrash most where ground is liable
To be kicked up - pungent, earthy.

Groundsmen mow the cricket square, till
Contrasting green Regency stripes
Show; then stand on club-house steps.
There, they think of matches, and shrill
Appeal shouts about petty gripes -
Then tea and the team's homeward footsteps.

Gillian C Fisher

STREET LIFE

I walked the streets of London
Because I had no home
My landlord had just kicked me out
To roam the streets alone
But as I turned a corner
I thought my time had come
When I bumped into a maniac
Who had a tiny gun
But then right out of nowhere
A man was by my side
Trying to protect me
From this other guy
And after he had punched him
He grabbed me by the hand
Then led me through an alleyway
That really looked so grand
At first I felt so frightened though
In case I'd have to pay
Not in actual money
But in another way
But then my fears all disappeared
As when we reached the door
I recognised a lady there
I'd met just once before
They really were so helpful
And treated me so kind
So I hope if you're in trouble too
You'll meet some friends like mine,.

Merilyn Gulley

TOO LATE

It was late in the evening as the teenager's footsteps
Echoed through the graffiti-daubed shopping precinct.
To his troubled mind the shadows all around him,
Looked like prehistoric monsters, long extinct.
The wild thoughts inside his head refused to go,
As a scrawny cat passed by on his nightly prowl.
While a pair of eyes in a nearby optician's window!
Stared out at him from a bronze sculptured owl.

A strong icy wind swept empty beer and Coke cans,
Up against a metal shop window shuttering.
From some obscure doorway he heard the sound,
Of loud incomprehensible muttering.

The teenager found what he was looking for!
A large discarded box that had been passed by
Then he smelt the nearby obnoxious drain,
Which told him the reason why.
He pulled the threadbare army greatcoat he wore,
His only protection from the wintry blast.
Up around his shoulders, thinking how the adventure,
Of the open road, had long since passed.

Spending the nights wrapped in old newspapers,
Lucky if he found a barn in some farmer's field.
Always trying to find the kind of warmth,
That his drink and drugs could not yield!

As the temperature dropped he thought about tomorrow,
It would be Christmas Eve, he would find a phone.
Then he could let everyone know he was returning,
Back to his family, to the friends he had known.
A road sweeper found him the following morning,
The last occupied box as a nearby clock struck eight.
He dialed for help from a phone kiosk close by,
Had the teenager made his call? Was it now too late!

N Plant

POLITICIANS' PROMISES

When every huddled beggar
on the street, hungry, old, homeless
sitting in a doorway, or against a wall
opens out a lap-top issued to the deprived,
in lieu of life, lights up a waiting screen,
a machine, promising to fly us to the skies,
over continents and seas
speedily on the super-highway
we'll know that the millennium's arrived.

Tap-tap-tap cold fingers
calling up magic pictures
on flickering screens, promising
a future of glorious, gracious
living. A niche in the power
of corporate capitalism,
a glut of information
for the houseless and the starving
for the jobless and the underpaid.
For all of us a golden age until -
energy fades.

Sheila Lahr

UN-SOCIETY

When did it all begin to happen?
These thoughts within my brain, which I am thinking,
and am I right or am I wrong, and for how long,
and am I really sane?
Because I wanted revolution,
and the fall of institution, but look where that has landed me!
For when I am lying in my cardboard box,
I know that I'm not free,
oh how I want to be free, free as the birds,
free as the stars in the sky,
but I know that can't happen, I know why,
for I've become part of un-society.
And thinking in confusing terms,
is caused by dis-establishment,
because I don't know who, or what I am,
and I don't know if I came or if I went.
But I know there's only one way out,
a new life is my only claim, to be, free,
and for the state my mind, my body's in,
there's only one to blame,
this nowhere life of un-society!

David Gebbie

LIFE IN THE STREET

How did I come this far down the social scale
And how much further do I have to go?
I had my chances, some say.
But do they really know?
I didn't always have to keep my pitch
By the warm air vent, to sleep.
Or to live the life of my chosen ease
According to some, who think they know.

I tried, I really did, to find a home
But no-one wanted to know me and my way of life
Except my dog. And now we share our food and shelter.
Left-over tourist food from the capital's bins.
With hunger gnawing away from within
It tastes like the best you have ever had.
On cold nights we curl up together in a doorway. He's warm
We live in fear of being moved on but that's our life.

One day perhaps I will kick this habit of being free
Of drifting in city streets and parks
But then, will anyone really want to know me?
I have my pals now among the down and outs (like me)
A friendly grin, a shared experience, a mutual thought.
Will being respectable mean so much?
It's been so long since my dignity mattered to anyone but me
And my faithful friend. Old Shep.

Iris Sheridan

OPERA

He hums an out of tune misbegotten Puccini aria
In his fat little port drenched head,
His fat little money-stroking hands covered
With expensive, genteel, stupid white gloves
And his expensive, genteel mind far away
From the rough edges of reality.
He just cannot, with his cushioned myopic mind,
See them, imagine them or, for one minute
Allow them the grace of being alive,
The freedom to breathe his little portion of air,
Or the chance to share one penny of his millions.
For he is a fat cat,
A privileged few, and they are the shame
Of his blindness, the blight on his wealth
And the victims of his success.
As he struts with belly billowing outwards,
Opera bound, they squirm in supermarket packing boxes,
Faces pinched with icicle fear,
Lungs choked with car fumes
And souls without the decency of recognition.
But still he intones his Puccini,
And clawing hands outstretched fail to make any inroad
Between him and his music.

Mary Jane Hanscomb

WHY?

I huddle on my thin blanket and wonder why
Why did I do it?
I lay on the cold, stony floor and I wonder why
Where did it all go wrong?
People walk past, the world drifts by I wonder why
Why don't they care?
The few pence collected in my tin why?
Why did it ever get this bad?
The man next to me old and drunk why?
Why did I think I could cope?
My home, a faded vision, another world why?
Why did I leave the comfort and love?
I wanted the freedom I wanted the fun why?
Now I have nothing
Why did I go?

Janine Green (14)

ON THE ROAD

Quite often I see her
She's walking fast
Bound for who knows where
She walks past our house
On the road to nowhere, from nowhere
She always seems to be walking in the same direction
Her feet are bare, her clothes in tatters
But she always looks like she's got a purpose
There's a smile on her face
There's a bounce in her step
Is she in a continuous time loop
Destined forever to walk the same path?
From nowhere to nowhere else
Where does she go?
She walks too fast for me to ask
On and on forever
Does she never rest?

Maria Hargraves

DOSSIN' WID DAVE

Twelve o'clock comes around again
We're on the streets once more
Me and Jack the lad
Hell we must've walked miles
Got blisters to prove it
Keep an eye open for blue lights
Found an old house to kip in
Couldn't sleep for a while
Eventually dozed off
Woke up feeling crucified
Staggered out into the morning light
Found a shop open
Fumbled in my pocket for small change
Devoured a bag of crisps
Clutched my bottle of milk
Sat down
Smoked a fag
Got up
Walked on

Jim Price

MAN OF THE STREETS

I saw him raking through a litter bin
To seek some bread to eat.
Dressed in rags, his body thin,
And tatty boots upon his feet.

This dreg of human society
Lives in a world without pity.
To wander the road is his priority.
He is the shame of a blinkered city!

His only solace is a bottle of meths,
When his mind is numbed by the cold.
How can a man sink to these depths
Is his life a story to be told.

Was he born to the poorest of poor.
And never given the choice
To pass through a far better door
And have cause to laugh and rejoice.

Brenda Beere

THE STORM

Hungrily devouring a measly meal of discarded junk food
huddled in my cardboard shelter, shivering cold
silently watching grey storm clouds gather
ragged multiple layers of tattered clothing
sole protection from the rigours of winter
oppressive atmosphere, electric charged
drawing broken boxes closer, tighter
sealing cracks and holes with scavenged polythene
first heavy raindrops spatter atop my makeshift home
downpour, deluge, wetting, soaking
incandescent lightning flashes silhouette my soggy refuge
thunder booms overhead echoing in my ears
leaking rain trickles slowly down my neck
seeking out exposed flesh, seeping, drenching
emerge from the flooded remnants, storm abated
body dripping, feet squelching, freezing cold

Chris Birkitt

MACHO

Out here and hanging about
don't care that people shout
and yell at me to clear off -
I'm not scared of stuck-up toffs.
Got good mates, who stand by me
when life gets tough and I'm in need.

On the street I feel I'm free
no-one there to nag at me.
No-one wants me for my loot -
just to have a friend for pool
or for the times when life's amiss
or when it's raining - that's the pits.

But I admit, when tired and beat
and looking for a dry retreat,
my head starts racing to the time
when maybe I won't have a dime,
and maybe I'll need more than beer
to make me sleep and chase those fears.

It scares me, when I see my chums
push grass or worse to spaced-out bums.
I get to thinking of the days
when home meant something more than faze,
more than parents' screamed insults,
somewhere I was warm and loved.

Dunno what that means now. I
now have to show my macho side
and laugh at those who fall in love
or join that * * * * * * * rat-race stuff.
We losers know a thing or two -
don't worry, 'spect I'll make it through.

Susan Biggin

DISAPPEARED OPPORTUNITIES

Homeless drifters and vagrants for years have always been around
Openly living in shop doorways today they can be found.
Many years ago they would have joined the army, out of view.
Extracted casual work from farmers or helped build roads too.
Less and less unskilled labour is needed in this technical age
Employers want people with motivation at every stage.
Sadly for some endless previous problems at school and home
Snowballed, with a bleak future they would continually roam.

Mary E Beale

UNDERGROUND

Today another day, full of grey
Clouds gather far above my head,
Rolling thunder, lightning forks towards the earth,
And leaves me wet, forlorn and stark,
Longing for a shelter, a blanket some friend
Or fellow being to share my fearful lot.
No-one seems to know I'm here
So I will not cry out in my hour of need,
Just find another hedge, another barn
To rest my soaking, swollen shabby shell
A layabout to some, more likely caused
By some misguided law, distorted by a bureaucrat,
Condemned to limbo, a vagrant of the underground,
Accused of things beyond control . . .
Of things, God knows I did not do.

Liz Dicken

LIFE ON THE STREET

It's hard to imagine life on the street
It really seems so sad
To sleep out under the stars at night
Even when the weather is bad

To raid the cities' litter bins
In an attempt to find something to eat
Wearing second hand clothes upon their backs
And odd shoes on their feet

Begging money from the passer-by
To feed a habit or buy a drink
There's nothing these poor people won't do
It really makes you think

The bag lady with her possessions
In her carriers at her side
She roams the streets day after day
She has no place to hide

The hostel is quite a luxury
For all the down and outs
Giving comfort to the wayward
The addicts, tramps and louts

Where do these people come from?
They must have once had a home
Has life just got too much for them?
And have left to be on their own.

I'm glad that I'm not one of them
To live like that I could not bear
Going from shop doorway to another
Their life just going nowhere

L A Brown

HOME SWEET HOME

Another cardboard box rape,
She squeezes, the twenty pound note tight inside her head.
Dreams of other times, warm lands, joyful plans,
A quick rush to whiskey man,
Helps the darkness fade today.

A newspaper of vomit, spreads and spills its views
The wind blows upon the cardboard box doorway.
As the next member of society's breed,
Carefully, silently screams, his way into street life land,

She loved once, a fairy tale ago,
But somebody slew the dragon,
So she just had to go,

Now tomorrow's faceless rapes,
Pay and pave the way, for angel wings,
And perhaps better things in God's little A-Z street plan,
Until then, home, sweet home,
Is cardboard box land

Terry Simmons

THE REAL CRIMINALS

'Crime is on the increase,' we always read
We complain about the youths of today
But what about the other side
Let me have my say
Everyone has given up on me
So why should I try?
Education's turned its back on me
But you didn't hear me cry
Instead I turned to drink and drugs
And people ask me why
But if I have no hope, no friends
Why shouldn't I try?
They make me forget I have no love
They make me feel free
They make me happy for a while
They make me forget I'm me
And while I'm not me
And my mind is no longer my own
I do crazy things
That I cannot condone
Kill a kid, stab a man
Burgle a house, steal a van
I can't remember a thing
When I come down
All I can remember is
That for a while I was as happy as a clown
So you see
Crime isn't because I'm a naughty kid
It's because I'm not loved, I have no faith
And you are all the real reason I did what I did.

Lindsey Brown

STAND AND STARE

A lonely figure lies in a huddle
Covered in blankets, one draped in a puddle
An empty bottle by his side
This man has nowhere to hide,
Open to life's bitterness
And people's unpleasantness.
At this man we just stand and stare
For we don't care
But what if we were he
What would our fate be?

Trevor Read

LIFE'S SYMPHONY

The clicking of the door handle,
The turning of the key,
Vast silence in the music hall,
That hangs so heavily.
Descend the steps that echo,
Rebounding, sounds beyond,
Away into the lamp-edged streets,
Blending within its song.

Percussion from the horse's iron,
On craggy cobbled paves.
Accompanied by sharp commands,
As the whip is lashed with rage.
Stern creeks, from ageing timbers,
As the wheels screeched to their plight.
Just a chord within a symphony,
Of a song throughout the night.

Unceasing, muffled, lyrics,
Combine, tear tunes of the young.
From dark corners, groan the begging cries,
Whilst the cheery, drunkard, sang.
Nimbly, tapped dainty heels,
As falls the blind man, frail,
All in verse, within the song,
That tells a weary tale.

Giggles of the fancy maid,
As the young squire, doffs his hat.
Compelling instant thoughts of grandeur,
And flirting chit-a-chat.
A chorus, known by many,
Joyous tones, of laughter gay;
Through the song of evening,
And on into the day.

Sara Russell

OLD JOE

Poor old Joe, he had nowhere to go, nowhere to call his own.
He'd sit on the pavement with downcast eyes,
Murmuring thanks for the few coppers thrown
On his bundle of rags, he was always alone.
And every evening, come what may,
He would move himself to a shop doorway.
This was no great logistical feat.
There was only himself and a bundle of rags,
A bottle, and maybe a bite to eat.
Apparently Joe was of very good family,
The type well accepted in any community,
He still had a brother and sister who lived close by.
Each claimed him to be on their conscience, true,
Though, of course, they were slightly embarrassed too.
He dropped out as a lad, a promising lad,
Mum said 'Mark my words, he'll be back before long.
He'll see his mistake.' Mum was wrong.
One night last spring, unexpectedly,
A frost came out of a clear night sky.
Joe hated the cold, as you might expect,
And, weakened by years of drink and neglect,
His sleep was a sleep of death that night,
And he never said goodbye.
His brother and sister, generously,
Marked the end of his life with dignity,
With a funeral appropriate to the family name.
Now it seems to console them to ponder long
On the hows and the whys and the what went wrong?
They have both shed tears, but, truth to tell.
They're a little upset, but pretty relieved as well.

Joan Isbister

CARDBOARD CITY

I curl up tight in a tiny ball
and try to pretend I'm not here at all,
as my toes freeze through the hole in my socks
and the rain pelts down on my cardboard box
the crescendo of noise as I cover my head,
dear Lord what I'd give for a nice warm bed.

Cold, tired and hungry but what can I do?
Whatever I try it's catch twenty-two.
To get a job I need a home,
a bath, clean clothes and a brush and comb.
But with no money to pay the rent,
I thank the Lord for my cardboard tent.

I'm not alone there are hundreds more,
here in cardboard city and on the floor
rolled up in paper are hundreds too,
like me who don't know what to do.
We beg enough for soup or tea
but drugs and prostitution are not for me.

As days turn to weeks and months to a year
and my desperation turns to anguish and fear,
I'm smelly and dirty, cold and hungry too,
so just thank God that it isn't you.
For nobody cares if I live or die,
as I hide in my box and break down and cry.

You see, I can't go home because nobody cares,
they are all too busy with their own affairs.
My parents split and mum's boyfriend's a cad,
no way can he take the place of my dad.
So now I've no home, no place for my bed
except in this box, I'd be better off dead.

Irene A Keeling

A SOMEONE . . .

the eyes - close - the mind travels
darkness falls
thoughts unravel - but not completely

screaming out for love - screaming for the pain
screaming for the wait - screaming for someone

for someone -
a scream that goes unheard
around the world and back again

a need that goes unmet -
a continuing warmth that's never felt

a mind out its head - not for this time
it never stops - but nevertheless
a friend to this world - a friend of mine

the eyes - close - they always do
and will continue to but
always with a smile on the face
as she falls from grace

a prayer - a person - as someone who needs
a someone whose screams - a someone
whose meaning

is silent

ssh . . .

Jacqueline Miller

SONNET

If I died tomorrow, would anybody care?
Would they wake up in the morning to discover I'm not there?
Another corpse: another bleak statistic in book,
A nameless nobody, for whom no-one will take a second look.

Once I had a home and friends, a place to lay my head;
Now I find a doorway with a pavement for a bed.
Once I had a job and prospects, good food every day,
Now I only walk the streets to pass the hours away.

I can't draw dole because I have no permanent address;
Without the cash, how can I find a way out of the mess?
I'm trapped inside a vicious vortex, unable to break free,
Reduced to begging for a crust - or just a cup of tea.

Loneliness is crippling, it increases black despair:
If I died tomorrow, who is there left to care?

June Steele

DON'T GO IT ALONE

I can imagine how street life can be,
Wandering and looking aimlessly
For somewhere to lay your tired-out body,
After looking for work decidedly dodgy.

Feeling all alone and nobody cares
Whether you eat, or sleep on the stairs.
Why leave home from safe and loving care
When there's so much dark desolation there.

The saying goes 'it looks greener the other side of
the fence,'
But we know that is only pretence.
So bring up your families to love their homes
And help to stop so many going it all alone.

Evelyn M Harding

CARDBOARD CITY

Here I live in cardboard city
Regrets I've only a few
Begging money from people's pity
But once I was just like you
A long time ago a job I had
And life was grand just swell
Then business went from good to bad
Now cardboard city's where I dwell
Since then I've tried to gain employment
They looked at my clothes old and frayed
And much to the employer's enjoyment
Explained begging wasn't their trade
So I decided to leave the rat race
Leave all the headaches behind
Just me and my shabby old suitcase
And no debts to play on my mind
So I'll stay in cardboard city
The best move that I ever made
Begging money from nice people's pity
And weekly my dole money's paid

Les Worthington

CHURCHGOERS

I stand and watch
Late on a Sunday night.
The people emerge from church
Into the dark from the light.

The people chatter happily,
The children are bonny and well fed.
Noisily they mingle with the crowd.
Soon they will be home in bed.

How joyous to receive salvation,
Their shallow souls purified once more,
Weaving their way towards the line of cars,
A flick of the remote opens a door.

The night is my cover,
The step my pillow and my bed.
Tiredness fills my weary heart,
Numbness fills my head.

One humble King
Breathed His last upon a tree.
They feel they have touched Him today.
Oh, why have you forsaken me?

Jan Chandler

NONENTITY TO NONENTITY

The diverse streams of life -
for the nomad
the poverty ripple -
his grades washed away
on the tidal-wave
of Monopoly!

His diploma -
a tatty blanket
with cardboard surrounds,
framed in 100%
carat pavement
of Equality!

The Westminster counterpart
rides high on his own Crest -
26% rise
with perks -
his daytime fare
manipulating the ripples!

He tosses them ever closer
towards the sands
to scavenge -
to fade from
Civilisation!

Mary Skelton

THE HOMELESS MAN

His past is unknown,
As he faces his plight,
No bitterness is shown,
On another cold night,
His aim is to survive,
At living it rough,
Just staying alive,
Is in itself enough,
A bin full of scraps,
Infested with flies,
Though it's food perhaps,
For the man with sad eyes,
He has nowhere to go,
No future to plan,
A life full of woe,
For the homeless man.

Martin Westcott

NOT YOUR PROBLEM?

You stare as you pass by,
no smile, no pity for me
never looking into my eyes,
scorn and contempt in yours.

I make you feel uncomfortable,
a blot on your perfect landscape
you may drop 50 pence into my box,
but with your hand, never your heart.

You do not understand my torment,
I am in the depths of despair,
in the darkest pit of life,
I cannot climb out of that pit.

I am tired, weak and afraid,
do not mock me with
your superior airs and glances,
I need your help and understanding.

Yes I am dirty, I do beg,
sleep in a box, I am also
a son, a grandson, a brother
I could be yours, one day.

I want to go home,
the prodigal son returned,
to be welcomed, loved, forgiven,
but not today, maybe tomorrow.

P A Edmondson

THE ROAD OF LOST SOULS

You can always be certain of finding him there,
Sitting alone in The Road of Lost Souls,
Wearied of life, with many a care
In his heart and his clothes full of holes.
Yet whatever the weather his face wears a grin
And he shares the little he can;
Generous and giving, honest from within,
You have a good friend for life in this man.
Ignore the stench which ever seems to shroud him
And disregard the filth in which he lies,
Rather see him for who he is and talk to him,
Realise the warmth and wit in those shrewd eyes.
As the streetwalkers pass, plying their trade,
Old Tommy shares a joke and a friendly word
With all. Many times over he is repaid
By their laughter and friendship. You may have heard
That The Road of Lost Souls is a dark, gloomy place
Where the outcasts of life are forced to remain,
Mutilated of body and grotesque of face,
Not a thread of dignity are they able to retain.
Yet Tommy wants only to be left alone
To pass the remainder of his days
Resting in a road where his pillow is a stone
And though some people pass, no-one stays.
Pity him not, for Tommy would say, he is luckier than most.
No longer must he rise at dawn each day
And listen to the chattering, idle boast
Of those he once mistakenly called friends.
He has freedom of choice, of word and of deed,
Freedom from all until the time his life ends.

Kathryn Walter

OH TO BE HAPPY!

Oh to be happy, everything all right,
The moon in the sky, shining bright in the night,
The sun during day, giving heat all around,
Oh to be happy, that would be sound.

Why can't I be happy, live in eternal bliss,
With love and passion, a person to kiss,
I'll never be happy in my cardboard box,
I have nothing to give, not even my socks.

Oh to be happy, I wish for that day,
When people will turn round and look my way,
Not sneer when I smile with my toothless grin,
Nor turn their backs, when I'm on the gin.

I'm a down and out, that don't make me queer,
I'm only a baglady, you've nothing to fear.

Kate Brown

STREET LIFE

Do you think when you rip open a large parcel
And take all the wrapping apart
That the box could have been someone's shelter
And the wrapper could warm up their heart
We buy all our papers for knowledge
Where they need our paper for heat
So the box they can use for their blanket
While the paper is warming their feet
Life on the street is not easy
It's hard to keep begging for food
So if passing just throw them a penny
As life for them cannot be good
It may not be their choosing
Sleeping rough and cold every night
While some of us are born lucky
Others don't see the light
No doubt they often sit and wish
They had a home to go
But mother nature wasn't good to them
So the street is all they know
A piece of bread and water
Could see them through the day
After all they are still human
So don't turn your head away.

Dinah Holt

RETRO

Street wise and hip
polished and glib
ship-shape and dandy
punching from the lip.

An accent assumed
from seventies telly
Regan and the Flying Squad
Arfur and Terry.

It's Waterloo sunset
morning noon and night
picking a path through
the dusk of eternal hindsight.

Andrew Ayres

STREET LIFE

You open your weary eyes
You've survived another night
People rush by around you
Yet you wonder
How you'll kill your time,
Make the day pass quickly
The odd kindly stranger
May offer a sympathetic smile
Or a little change
Yet they don't care enough
They can't understand
You've nothing left
But dreams and wishes
How did it all come to this?
Will it ever end?
The day crawls by
As you search for a sleeping place
And blink the tears from your eyes
Today like yesterday
Tomorrow like today.

Maria Brown

STREET WISE KIDS

Street wise kids, that's what they're called,
the ones who hang around the infant school,
lounging about and sitting on the wall.
Walking about the streets of their home patch,
thinking no way can they be matched,
wanting to be the coolest dude,
to be seen to have the meanest mood.

Sussing out the best places to hit,
the best bikes to be nicked,
to say what is kosher, or not,
when really all they are, are . . .
. . . little shits.

The average age is thirteen plus,
they are foul mouthed little sods,
all are known by the local PC Plod.
With a string of warnings, never heeded,
a tougher line is definitely needed.
But they know the law inside out,
know we can't give the a clout, or
threaten them, never mind shout!

Like brazen hussies they stand there,
and flout their attractions and wares,
of stolen watches, tapes and videos,
enticing, cajoling the younger kids,
offering them a share. They look up to
the gang with admiration in their eyes,
see how to leer, sneer and jeer, see
how to make others look at them with fear,
and so their foot is on the first rung of
the ladder, the beginning of their career.

J Marlow

THE ONLOOKER

He lives on the outside,
this man of shattered dreams.

Each day his eyes
peek over barriers at
lives that move unhindered
and sting his pincushion heart.

He loves their satin wares,
but never fortune shares.

David Stockdale

HOME

Today he offered coke
Yesterday it was E.
I refused, I always do,
I never have the money.

She spent last night
In a different man's bed:
She cried, she always does,
But it brings back the bread.

The Star as a pillow
The Sun at our feet,
The girls on page three
He rips out to keep.

They haven't found us, yet
On our latest site,
But they're coming, I smell them
And we'll give up the fight.

'Move on, move on,'
We're health hazards all,
And gone is the summer
And here is the fall.

We'll get through the winter
If we beg and we cheat,
If we go it together,
If we steal what we eat.

In this wide world that hates me
I'm all alone.
Doesn't seem much
But it's what I call home.

Elizabeth Harrin

INFORMATION

We hope you have enjoyed reading this book - and that you will continue to enjoy it in the coming years.

If you like reading and writing poetry drop us a line, or give us a call, and we'll send you a free information pack.

Write to :-

**Poetry Now Information
1-2 Wainman Road
Woodston
Peterborough
PE2 7BU**